DONALD SULTAN

A Print Retrospective

Barry Walker

The American Federation of Arts

in association with

RIZZOLI
NEW YORK

This catalogue has been published in conjunction with *Donald Sultan: A Print Retrospective*, an exhibition organized and circulated by the American Federation of Arts. The exhibition is a project of ART ACCESS, a program of the AFA with major support from the Lila Wallace-Reader's Digest Fund.

EXHIBITION TOUR

Lowe Art Museum
Coral Gables, Florida
September 17–November 8, 1992

Butler Institute of American Art
Youngstown, Ohio
December 6, 1992–January 31, 1993

Museum of Fine Arts, Houston
Houston, Texas
June 26–August 22, 1993

Sheldon Memorial Art Gallery
Lincoln, Nebraska
January 30–March 27, 1994

Madison Art Center
Madison, Wisconsin
May 28–July 23, 1994

Orlando Museum of Art
Orlando, Florida
August 20–October 15, 1994

The American Federation of Arts, a non-profit organization, is committed to broadening the public's knowledge and appreciation of the visual arts by organizing traveling exhibitions of fine arts and media arts and to providing specialized services that strengthen visual arts institutions.

© 1992 by The American Federation of Arts
Published by the American Federation of Arts
41 East 65 Street, New York, New York 10021
and Rizzoli International Publications, Inc.
300 Park Avenue South
New York, New York 10010

92 93 94 95 96 / 10 9 8 7 6 5 4 3 2 1

Printed in Hong Kong
Library of Congress Cataloging-in-Publication Data
Walker, Barry, 1945–
    Donald Sultan: a print retrospective/Barry Walker.
    p.   cm.
    Includes bibliographical references.
    ISBN 0-8478-1591-9
    1. Sultan, Donald—Exhibitions. I. Sultan, Donald.
II. American Federation of Arts. III. Title.
NE539.S85A4   1992   92–14630
769.92—dc20   CIP

Publication Coordinator, AFA: Michaelyn Mitchell
Design and typography: Russell Hassell
Editor: Scott Gutterman
Photographer: Ken Cohen
Printer: South Sea International Press, Ltd.

Cover: no. 47
Photos page 4 and 6: Donald Sultan, December 1984.
Courtesy Brenda Zlamany

CONTENTS

In his career as a printmaker, Donald Sultan has produced an extensive, varied, and powerful body of work. This exhibition provides an eye-opening view of the full range of his graphic work, which encompasses great variety and richness in subject matter, technique, and scale. Embracing both abstract and representational approaches, Sultan's prints—like his paintings and drawings—are alluring and enigmatic.

Thanks must go first and foremost to the artist himself, who not only agreed to loan all the prints for this exhibition but was courteous, cooperative, and patient throughout the development of the project. Sultan's studio assistants have also been extremely helpful, in particular, Jane Creech, who has been unfailingly pleasant and professional.

We are indeed fortunate to have enlisted the talents of noted print scholar Barry Walker, who has served as guest curator for the exhibition. Mr. Walker's selection presents a complete survey of Sultan's prints, and his catalogue essay elucidates their place in Sultan's overall work.

Here at the AFA, the entire staff must be acknowledged for all its efforts. In particular, Andrew Spahr, curator of exhibitions; Michaelyn Mitchell, head of publications; Julie Min, exhibition scheduler; Carol Farra, registrar; Kathleen Flynn, former associate registrar; and Andrea Crane, publications assistant. As ever, David Farmer, director of exhibitions, Bob Workman, assistant director of exhibitions, and Jillian Slonim, public information director, have made important contributions.

Russell Hassell has produced a handsome and fitting design for the exhibition catalogue that we hope will serve as a useful resource for both scholars and collectors alike.

Serena Rattazzi
Director, The American Federation of Arts

DONALD SULTAN

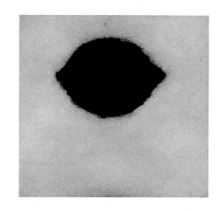

Donald Sultan's images, particularly in his graphic work, are simultaneously representational and abstract, comfortingly familiar and oddly, almost eerily distancing. His work is rigorously intellectual in its attack on pictorial problems, yet elusively romantic in terms of ostensible subject matter. It is premodern in its buried references, modern in its geometry, and postmodern in its irony.

Sultan came of age when Minimalism and Conceptualism were the dominant artistic modes, and he has certainly been influenced by their systemic methods of image construction. His approach to imagery, however, denies the Minimalist tenet that forms are created from a predetermined series of marks on a grid and that any single grid unit contains all the information necessary to imply the whole.

In the construction of his paintings, Sultan incorporates aspects of Minimalism and Process Art. His format is that of the Minimalist grid; industrial linoleum tiles form the basic building blocks of his support structures. The foot-square vinyl tiles are backed with Masonite, which is in turn backed with a four-foot-square sheet of plywood bolted to a stretcher. Sultan generally combines these basic units in groups of two or four. When the tiles are covered with a skin of butyl rubber, a tarlike substance used in roofing, the surface is finally prepared. After establishing the contours of the image in chalk, he cuts, scrapes, or burns off the butyl with a blowtorch. He then rebuilds the surface with plaster and applies color with a sponge or rag. This method relates his work to Process Art and, as a subtractive way of working, is allied more to printmaking than to traditional painting.

Sultan's work is always concerned, on some level at least, with recognizable imagery. In the late 1970s and early 1980s, therefore, critics attempted to lump his work with that of the

New Image painters.[1] His style was too elusive, however, to fit conveniently or consistently with even such a loosely defined school, whose members advocated a return to representation of a more intensely felt variety than the depersonalized images of the Pop artists. Sultan's images were too remote and seemingly serene to be a part of a movement that, as the decade wore on, became identified as Neo-Expressionism.

Probably it is not yet possible to establish Sultan's exact place within the context of his peers. It is, however, illuminating to reexamine his imagery within the continuum of art history. His approach is distinctly postmodern in its ambiguity. The imagery is recognizable, but the flattened, overscale treatment is nonillusionistic. One can divide Sultan's paintings into two categories: "event" paintings and still lifes. The former are landscapes, usually urban or industrial, often derived from newspaper photographs. They are dark paintings that depict everyday disasters such as fires or nearly unimaginable ones such as nuclear meltdowns. When figures appear in these paintings, Sultan eliminates any specificity that would indicate personality or character; featureless, they are purely generic.

In the seventeenth and eighteenth centuries, a hierarchical system based on categories of imagery was applied to paintings. The highest category, considered the most ambitious and noble, was history painting, which encompassed images that illustrated the Bible and mythology, as well as those depicting significant historical events. In this age of instant visual communication, Sultan's event paintings fall roughly within the category of history paintings. By transforming an ordinary newspaper photograph into an eight-foot-square painting stripped of all but the most essential details, he imparts a monumental, heroic quality to images that were, in their original form, disposable.

At the other end of the hierarchy of imagery was still-life painting, the depiction of objects both natural and man-made in a deliberately composed interior or nonspecific setting. Still life was held in such low esteem partly because it was intended for a bourgeois clientele. It elevated imagery that would have been mere decoration in a palace to the position of art in the homes of merchants and bankers. It is interesting to note that flower painting, a subgenre of still life, first flourished in the Netherlands at the time that trade in tulip bulbs was one of the main staples of the economy.

The Industrial Revolution and the advent of Modernism effectively destroyed the categories of hierarchy in painting. In the nineteenth century, still life evolved from the glorification of things, of possessions, into a genre imbued with the same seriousness of purpose as any other classification of painting. It became the principal subject of Cubism, the movement that first defined twentieth-century Modernism, and has remained a key classification in the recent history of image painting. Jasper Johns's American flags and Andy Warhol's soup cans are but two icons of recent art history that fall within the genre of still life. As contemporary examples, Sultan's lemon pictures are rapidly assuming the status of postmodern icons.

By selecting still life as the other major category of his mature paintings, Sultan positioned himself in line with the highest aspirations of Modernism. His still-life paintings are either monumental doubles or quadruples of the four-foot-square panels or what might be termed domestic in scale—one-foot-squares. Until very recently, the subject matter was generally limited to a few categories: vegetables, fruits, eggs, and flowers.

Any consideration of Sultan's unique work is incomplete without an examination of his drawings. They are also essential in any discussion of his aquatints, the most innovative aspect of his printed oeuvre, as the development of technique in each is inextricably related to the other. The drawings comprise an independent body of work rather than studies for paintings; they are mostly large-scale and highly finished. In the earlier ones he employed some graphite with charcoal, but the more recent ones, those executed since late 1983, are done in pure charcoal on paper.

The drawings of Sultan's mature career are also still lifes, and they share the paintings' subject matter. In these large black-and-white drawings, the subjects are greatly magnified and flattened. They invite a dual reading. Tulips and irises suggest the female figure; lemons imply schematized breasts; and eggs, testicles. The images are sometimes central, sometimes arbitrarily cropped. Sultan has acknowledged the influence of Georges Seurat's drawings,[2] in which the concern with nonspecific, unfixed edge is of equal value with that of form.

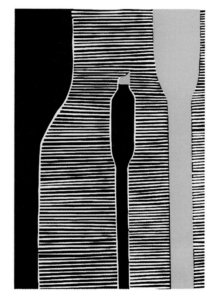

A discussion of Sultan's charcoal drawings leads inevitably to a comparison with his aquatints, as each medium has affected the other. He is best known as a printmaker for his black-and-white aquatints, but his range is much broader, having worked in every major graphic discipline.

In the tradition of the *peintre-graveur*, he has moved effortlessly back and forth between media, the innovations in one area informing those in the others. He has worked in lithography and block printing, but his principal graphic techniques now are screenprint and aquatint, and his attitude towards each is vastly different in a way not entirely explained by the quite different disciplines of each medium.

Sultan began making prints in 1978 at the urging of Robert Feldman, director of Parasol Press. As Sultan recalls it, "[Feldman] had seen the show I'd done at the New Museum of the black tar drawings, which were done with caulking guns. He said, 'You should really do some prints. You should do linoleum cutting.' Well, I didn't really want to do linoleum cutting, so he sent me to Crown Point Press, which was in Oakland at that time. I stayed two weeks out there and made a series of etchings called 'Water Under the Bridge,' and that started me in printmaking."[3]

"Water Under the Bridge" in many ways encapsulates Sultan's methods, as well as the evolution of his imagery. His way of working recalls Jasper Johns's often quoted dictum: "Take an object. Do something to it. Do something else to it."[4] The eight images that comprise "Water Under the Bridge," culled from forty plates Sultan executed in his two weeks at Crown Point Press, show how every aspect of an image, including the negative as well as the positive areas, is of equal pictorial weight and significance to him.

In this first series of prints, Sultan established the working methods he would employ in his intaglio work of 1979–80. Using all the basic methods of etching and engraving—hard-ground, soft-ground, drypoint, aquatint, scraping, and burnishing—he created a sort of primer on the medium. Although the sixth print in the series, *Iceberg/Boat Prow, March 25, 1979* (cat. no. 6), is executed in pure aquatint, the others are structured by line work. His edges at that time were much more clearly defined than in the later aquatints.

Many of the incidental characteristics of Sultan's paintings and drawings have been carried into the graphic work. He signs and annotates vertically along either the right or the left edge. Recently, he has begun, although not invariably, to place the edition number along the lower edge because his prints have so often been illustrated with the wrong orientation. He includes the date he finishes a work—always by month and year, sometimes by specific day—as part of the title.

For the images in "Water Under the Bridge," Sultan employed a system of cut-out linoleum templates that suggested a kind of multiple image-making. He called the cut-outs "puzzle pieces." "After I cut an image out of linoleum, I would turn it over and trace it and cut it, and it would become something else." All the individual titles in "Water Under the Bridge" are double titles, underscoring the duality of Sultan's images. Shifts of image orientation and scale of detail invite entirely new multiple readings. The relative statuses of negative and positive space are likely to reverse.

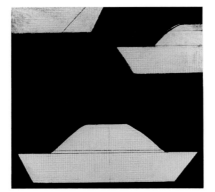

The first image in the portfolio, *Boat/Table, March 20, 1979* (cat. no. 1), shows an upended table that has become a boat. Of the series, Sultan observes, "They are the same images rearranged to make different things. For example, it starts with a black boat and it ends up with a cigarette. The cigarette is the space between the upturned table legs—which is the boat—and the horizon line. The boat is the same shape as the smokestack edge in the cigarette, and the pointed parts make the sailor hat. They are all kind of flipped in and out, so you have the sailor hats, the bows, the tables, the rooms, the boat prow and the iceberg, and a navel

and panties. All these different things came out of manipulating the edges of one image." The cigarette image, *Cigarette/Stack, March 28, 1979* (cat. no. 8), was first developed in this series and later appeared in a number of paintings. "I'll create images in prints and later translate them into paintings, and vice versa. But most of the graphic images were done first in prints." The above is true of the early intaglio work; it does not apply to the screenprints.

Sultan returned to Crown Point Press in February 1980, at which point he executed six new plates. The first was a set of three, "Smokers" (cat. nos. 9–11), which combined aquatint with drypoint, mezzotint, and hard-ground. The scale of the plates, each forty-two inches square, was much larger than that of the earlier series. Whereas all the prints in "Water Under the Bridge" were composed in a traditional format with a three-inch margin all around, those in "Smokers" were printed on sheets whose dimensions were one-half inch smaller than those of the plates. With their enlarged scale and lack of margins, these prints had the physical presence of paintings. For the single image *Canyon, Feb. 28, 1980* (cat. no. 12), Sultan enlarged the image *Building/Canyon, Feb. 28, 1980.*[5] The left part of the image evolved from *Half Hats and Whole, March 24, 1979* (cat. no. 4), with the orientation reversed and the image enlarged and cropped. If one turns the print upside down, the positive and negative areas reverse, thus putting a slightly different spin on more traditional field-ground problem pictures.

In the summer of 1982, Feldman succeeded in persuading Sultan to work on linoleum cuts with the printer Jaime Arnéra in Vallauris, France. Although the artist completed two portfolios, "Tramp Pictures—Cypresses and Stacks" (cat. nos. 13–17) and "Tramp Pictures—Irises" (cat. nos. 18–20), the experience was fraught with difficulty. Arnéra wanted to carve the blocks from drawings, but Sultan insisted on carving the blocks himself in a highly unorthodox way. "Those prints worked out because I did what you're not supposed to do. I left the linoleum out in the sun and used heat to soften it up. This turned out to be the perfect way to do it. If you get the linoleum soft enough, you can use a pencil on it, which I don't think anyone had ever done before. I was very happy with the prints finally."

Although Feldman had proposed the project, the linoleum cuts were published by Sultan's gallery at that time, Blum Helman, in collaboration with Carmen Giménez. Despite the contretemps with the printer, Sultan loved being in France and now spends every summer there, working in a studio that once belonged to Paul Signac.

The two "Tramp Pictures" series marked the end of the first phase of Sultan's graphic work. "Cypresses and Stacks" were the last landscape-related images in the prints, and "Irises" presaged the flower and still-life images that were to dominate the succeeding printed images. His innovations in linoleum-cut technique hinted at the tremendous breakthrough he was about to make in aquatint.

Sultan made his first black tulip aquatint as a frontispiece for a deluxe edition of a poetry collection, *Prayers and Sermons for the Stations of the Cross* by April Bernard. Working in the same six-by-four-inch format, he created the four plates comprising the portfolio "Black Tulips" (cat. nos. 21–24). In these small aquatints, Sultan established his new and revolutionary technique.

Ironically, in wanting to develop an intaglio technique that would approximate the look of his charcoal drawings

(by definition an additive process), Sultan found a way of working that related more to the subtractive methods he used in the tar paintings. He had the plates covered with resin, then removed the negative spaces by brushing the resin away with a soft Japanese brush or blowing it away through a glass tube. "I got the idea of making the prints from the charcoal drawings. I worked the charcoal a lot as powder, let it spread out over the paper, and then fixed it. One day I thought, 'Aquatint is already powder, so if you work it dry and don't melt it until you've made the images, instead of doing the reverse, you won't have hard edges.'"

This subtractive technique, rather like the mezzotint method of working from dark to light, enabled Sultan to achieve a fuzzy edge that was almost not an edge at all. It also allowed him to use highly controlled incidental marks in the negative areas of the image. Because of this technique, the "Black Tulips" have a mysterious quality that is at once sensual and sinister.

After the intimacy of the small "Black Tulips" plates, Sultan decided to try his new technique on a much enlarged scale. His next portfolios of four and two aquatints, both entitled "Black Lemons" (here represented by *Black Lemon, Nov. 28, 1984*, cat. no. 25), became the signature images of his printed work. Each plate measures sixty-two by forty-eight inches and is printed on sheets only one-half inch larger in each dimension.

Sultan's use of the lemon actually evolved from his tulip paintings and drawings. While viewing the Manet exhibition at the Metropolitan Museum of Art, he was struck by a small, late still life, *Lemon*, 1880–81 (Musée d'Orsay). He perceived the lemon as a tulip blossom flipped on its side. First in paintings, then in drawings, and finally in prints, the lemon became his iconic image in the mid-1980s.

Sultan's lemon images resonate because they operate on several levels simultaneously. They have the generic silhouette associated with the object, but not the mimetic depiction of texture and volume or, in the aquatints and drawings, the characteristic color. They are lemons, but at the same time, both more and less than lemons. The shape acts as a point of departure. Sultan creates visual and psychological tension by distorting the form through the properties of whatever medium he may be working in to the point that the lemon becomes almost a geometrically abstract form, yet still is identifiably a lemon. Just as Alberto Giacometti stretched the human form beyond mannerist elongation into a shape at once generic and mythic, so Sultan manipulates the lemon form into something ominous and mysterious while still retaining its mundane familiarity. In the drawings and especially in the aquatints, the edges of the lemons become so powdery and undefined that the images barely retain their integrity as objects.

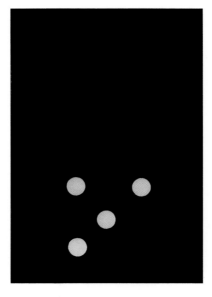

The problem with the large aquatints was that, with the resin not fixed, the plate could not be moved. The printer Jeryl Parker, who had left Crown Point Press, adapted his new studio in New York to accommodate Sultan's needs. They finally worked out a method whereby Sultan could work on the plate on a heat table that would eventually heat and fix the grains of resin. Parker constructed a huge aquatint box that was on rollers, so that it could drop the aquatint ground and be rolled away, leaving the resin undisturbed.

Sultan considers the aquatints an alternate and stylistically more advanced form of drawing. "I realized that I couldn't get the charcoal drawings as powdery as I wanted them. With charcoal you're adding, so you develop a technique to get your whites clean and your edges fuzzy. It gets really fussy. But with the prints, it's the reverse. In the aquatints, I solved the problem of how to make mysterious, intimate drawings without having to fuss with the damn thing."

In the "Freesias" portfolio (cat. nos. 30–33), Sultan returned to a hard-edge representation of flower stalks floating on a large, white field. The images look strangely like nineteenth-century portrait silhouettes. The anthropomorphic depiction of Sultan's flowers suggests that, in an iconic way, these are portraits too. In the portfolio of four large aquatints, "Lemons" (here represented by *Black Lemons and Egg, April 14, 1979*, cat. no. 34), he returned to the blurred edge that had become the hallmark of his intaglio prints.

Sultan made an imagistic breakthrough in his next set of eleven aquatints, "Female Series, April 1988" (cat. nos. 35–45). The images in this portfolio exist in no other medium in Sultan's work. They consist of details of the female figure isolated on six-by-four-inch plates set within much larger sheets; the latter characteristic provides an additional distancing effect to that already established by the cropping. "I got the idea from the prints in the tulip series. They looked so much like certain aspects of the female form that I thought I'd try it that way. The idea was to switch the two things around, to show that a flower could be very sexy, and something that would ordinarily be sexy could be more abstract."

The images of "Female Series" are indeed divorced from the whole range of Odalisque paintings, from Ingres through Manet to Matisse. The somewhat photographic quality also implies fragments of images from Muybridge's "Animal Locomotion" series. But because of Sultan's radical cropping, his figurative images in this series are treated more as still lifes than as figurative imagery. While the subjects are details of the human figure, the lack of context depersonalizes the images, forcing a reading of each form as pure object.

"To do these, I took a sheet of glassine and made a drawing on it, then turned the glassine over and traced it with charcoal. I placed the glassine on the plate and traced the outlines of the initial drawing. Next the aquatint was dropped on the plate. The odd thing is that you can see the drawing underneath the aquatint. It leaves a black shape, a trace line, but it doesn't leave anything on the plate. It was just straight printing. There was no hand other than mine involved and there was no stopout, just inking. It's just the plate, the powder, and the ink."

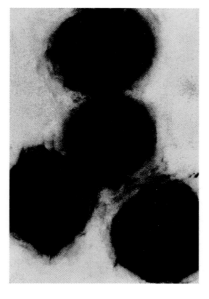

The "Female Series" is the closest to portraiture that Sultan has come in his work. He had always felt that he had nothing to add to that genre, especially in view of the work of Chuck Close and Andy Warhol.[6] His aquatint technique, however, has opened up possibilities that he has yet to explore. Sultan considers the "Female Series" a breakthrough in his work, although he is not sure where it will lead. "The difference with the 'Female Series' is the photographic quality of the work. The sideways nude, for instance, looks like a high-contrast photograph. I realized in doing the lemon prints that the white space could become like skin. It's grayish with pores, so I thought, 'This is natural for doing a figure.' In the 'Female Series,' I tried to make the white part fleshy, make it function actively instead of being just a void. It has a lot of different kinds of tonality that usually you can't get except by working photographically, or by a lot of mezzotint rocking and burnishing."

Sultan went on to work with the great French printer Aldo Crommelynck in Paris, making a series of four aquatints, "Lip Prints, Oct. 1989" (cat. nos. 52–55). For the two with black backgrounds, Sultan pressed his lips to resined plates, lifting the aquatint. In the case of the two prints with gray lips and lighter grounds, he greased his lips before applying them to the plates. The grease acted as a partial stopout, and the plates were etched with open-bite.

Sultan's next series of large aquatints was "Pomegranates" (cat. nos. 63–65), a set of three. The shapes evolved from the lemons, but are at once more decorative and more menacing, implying both exotic fruits and hand grenades. In one, two pomegranates are widely separated; in another, they nearly touch, the fuzzy edges almost blending into each other, yet the forms remain discrete. In the third, the forms of a group of pomegranates overlap. Although deliberately flat, their contours imply volume.

The most recent set of large-scale aquatints is "Morning Glories" (cat. nos. 66–68). These are huge prints, almost as big as the "Black Lemons," printed from sixty-by-forty-eight-inch plates on sheets measuring sixty-two by fifty. The three sheets constitute a triptych with the most densely worked image as the central panel. In this series, the center of each flower has been stopped out so that a perfect white circle appears in the middle of each bloom; the white circles seem to pop out of the velvety blackness. At the same time, the appearance of parts of the neutral support within the image insists on a flatness that the modeling contradicts. Because of their scale and the wonderfully fuzzy treatment of the edges, "Morning Glories" are among the most powerful prints Sultan has created. "I think the

'Morning Glories' prints are better than the drawings because they are more abstract and mysterious, more swimming in a way. The drawings are a little more decorative than I like."

Another issue in Sultan's printed oeuvre is the twelve-inch-square (composition size) screenprints in colors (cat. nos. 46–51). These prints are made at Watanabe Studio, a screenprinting shop in Brooklyn. They are derived directly from the small still-life and flower paintings through color separation. Whereas Sultan is totally involved in the creation of the aquatints, with the screenprints his role is passive. "I've worked with Jo Watanabe and his assistants a lot, so they know exactly what to do. I color proof at every stage, tinkering with the colors and the printing order."

Sultan's attitude toward the small screenprints is diametrically opposed to his attitude toward the aquatints. With the screenprints, he works in a traditional, essentially European mode in which a chromist color-separates from a unique work and draws the screens; the artist then fine-tunes the work. The screenprints also relate to the Japanese *ukiyo-e* style in which the artist creates a watercolor that highly trained artisans translate into woodblock prints. His attitude to the screenprints seems contradictory, particularly in light of his battles with Jaime Arnéra over his total involvement in the creation of the 1982 linoleum cuts. It is explained, however, by his perception of the medium as more technologically based than etching, and he accepts the intervention of artisans accordingly. Overall, the highly colorful screenprints are both more intimate and more exuberant than the large, brooding aquatints.

In 1990, Sultan's screenprints began to change. The previous year he had made three medium-sized (twenty-two-by-thirty-inch plate) aquatints, *Black Roses, Dec. 1989* (cat. nos. 56–58). In the screenprint *Black Roses, May 1990* (cat. no. 59), working with a related image, he enlarged the scale to thirty-four by fifty-five and one-half inches. In this, the color of the roses, as in the aquatints, is black; subtle, closely keyed colors form the gray-blue background. The scale and subdued colors of the screenprint set it apart from his earlier works in the medium.

The only major graphic medium that Sultan has not investigated to any significant degree is lithography. His one attempt at direct lithography (as opposed to photolithography) is a 1985 portfolio called "Warm and Cold" (cat. nos. 81–84). The project is essentially a *livre de luxe*; it was a collaboration between Sultan and his friend, the playwright David Mamet, to celebrate the births of their daughters. Sultan's images in "Warm and Cold" must be viewed as illustrations to Mamet's text, not as signature images. As illustrations, however, they are delightful, indicating a more playful side to Sultan's personality.

Sultan simply did not take to lithography. "The whole purpose of printing, in a way, is to try to keep the freedom of line, of drawing, in something that isn't free. The thing people like best about lithography is that they can make a wash with the acid and it looks like a wash. But it's not really a wash. It's a printed copy of a wash. So, I find drawings preferable."

The only other foray Sultan made into lithography was for a 1986 portfolio "Still Life with Pears and Lemons" (cat. nos. 26–28). Working in the one-foot-square format, he created an aquatint plate in black as the first image, a photolithograph in colors as the second, and an overprinting of the aquatint on the photolithograph as the third. The portfolio is somewhat odd and experimental, at once like and unlike Sultan's other graphic work.

In the last year, Sultan has added entirely new images to his still-life repertory. "Dominoes" (cat. nos. 60–62), a portfolio of three screenprints in the twelve-by-twelve inch format, derives from paintings of the same size. The domino images are almost pure geometry, black squares paired end to end with white circles on them. These screenprints are much more stark than his earlier ones in terms of imagery, but with more active surfaces. Each screen image combines glossy and matte inkings.

At roughly the same time he made the screenprints, Sultan released a portfolio, "Dominoes, Aug. 1990" (cat. nos. 69–72) of twenty-eight aquatints with etching. Each eleven-and-one-half-by-eight-inch plate represents a single, hard-edged tile. Sultan has played with the placement of the dots, locating some of them half off the edges. The white dots in these images relate to the much larger white dots in the "Morning Glories" series with its nonspecific edges.

The most recent portfolio is "Playing Cards" (cat. nos. 73–80), consisting of fifty-four aquatints representing the fifty-two playing cards and two jokers. The spades and clubs are printed in black, the hearts and diamonds in red. The pips on the cards are printed in Sultan's fuzzy style, their arrangement unlike that in any normal deck. *Ten of Diamonds* (cat. no. 76), for instance, has thirteen pips. Rather than drawing figures for the court cards, he created small symbols to denote the jack, queen, and king.

Playing cards have all sorts of references. Almost certainly the first Western prints were woodcut playing cards. They are often used for fortune telling, and certain cards, such as the ace of spades, the death card, connote bad luck or disaster. Picasso and Braque often incorporated playing cards into their still-life compositions; in this way Sultan once again aligns himself with historical Modernism.

Like all his still-life images, Sultan's "Playing Cards" evoke the essence of the objects, but modified and rearranged. Just try playing any card game with one of the facsimile decks. In both the drawings and aquatints, he has magnified the scale far beyond the cards' usual size. Working with the four suit symbols, he has created his own compositions, which function like musical variations on a theme. Each print refers to a specific card, but in terms completely of Sultan's own devising. Sultan first created the playing cards as charcoal (black suits) and Conté crayon (red suits) drawings. In the process of making the aquatint plates, however, the work changed considerably. Like the "Dominoes," "Playing Cards" are symbols, referring to themselves and a range of other sources.

All of Sultan's prints have been variations on the still-life tradition. He is ambivalent about translating event paintings into prints. "The event pictures have color in them. With etching, I have never been able to do color satisfactorily. I tried taking an image that I would use for an event picture and making a photogravure of it, then etching back into it with aquatint and seeing if I could take the photographic reproduction and alter it. But the gravure had such a strong bite on the plate that it just became muddy. I lost everything.

"Part of what characterizes the event pictures is that they are so tortured and dark and wild as paintings. The idea was really of experiencing something odd when you were there rather than looking at it. The fact that I'm reluctant to try to solve the problem of making event prints probably means that I don't think it's important."

What clearly is important to Donald Sultan is making images that work in terms of composition, technique, and ambiguity, and that walk a tightrope between formalism and content. "Basically I think I am a Minimalist. But I keep trying to add as much stuff as I can and still keep the sense."

Notes

1. *New Image Painting* was the title of an exhibition curated by Richard Marshall at the Whitney Museum of American Art. The ten artists included were Nicholas Africano, Jennifer Bartlett, Denise Greene, Michael Hurson, Neil Jenney, Lois Lane, Robert Moskowitz, Susan Rothenberg, David True, and Joe Zucker. See Richard Marshall, *New Image Painting*, exhibition catalogue (New York: Whitney Museum of American Art, 1978).

2. Barbara Rose, *An Interview with Donald Sultan by Barbara Rose* (New York: Elizabeth Avadon Editions/ Vintage Books, 1988), p. 57.

3. All quotes by Donald Sultan are from an interview between the author and the artist at the latter's studio, September 23, 1991.

4. Jasper Johns, "Sketchbook Notes," *Art and Literature* 4 (Spring 1965), p. 192.

5. *Donald Sultan: Prints 1979–1985* (Boston: Barbara Krakow Gallery, 1985). This volume has been an invaluable resource and the basis of the catalogue information for the pre-1986 work.

6. Rose, p. 48.

CATALOGUE

"Water Under the Bridge," 1979. Portfolio of eight aquatints. Each image printed from one 12 × 12 (30.5 × 30.5) copper plate on a sheet of 18 × 18 (45.7 × 45.7) Rives BFK paper (see exceptions, nos. 4 and 7). Edition: Forty-five, plus ten artist's proofs, three trial proofs, and one right-to-print proof. Printed by David Kelso and Hidekatsu Takada at Crown Point Press, Oakland, California. Published by Parasol Press, New York.

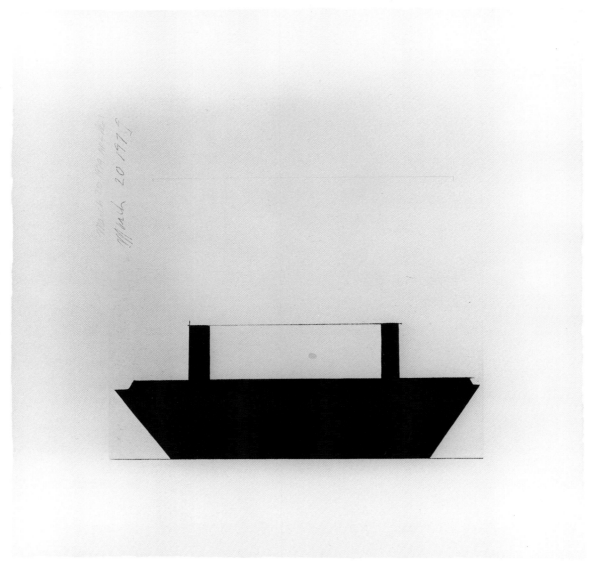

1. *Boat/Table, March 20, 1979.* Aquatint, hard-ground, soft-ground, and drypoint. Printed in black, gray, and oxidized white from two plates.

2. *Sailor Hats, March 21, 1979.* Aquatint with scraped and burnished areas, hard-ground, and drypoint. Printed in black from one plate.

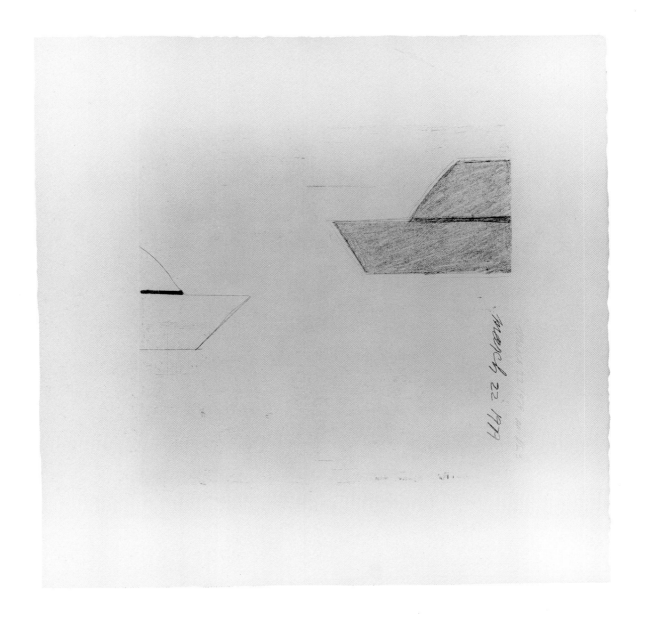

3. *Half Hats, March 22, 1979.* Soft-ground, drypoint, and hard-ground. Printed in black and gray from two plates.

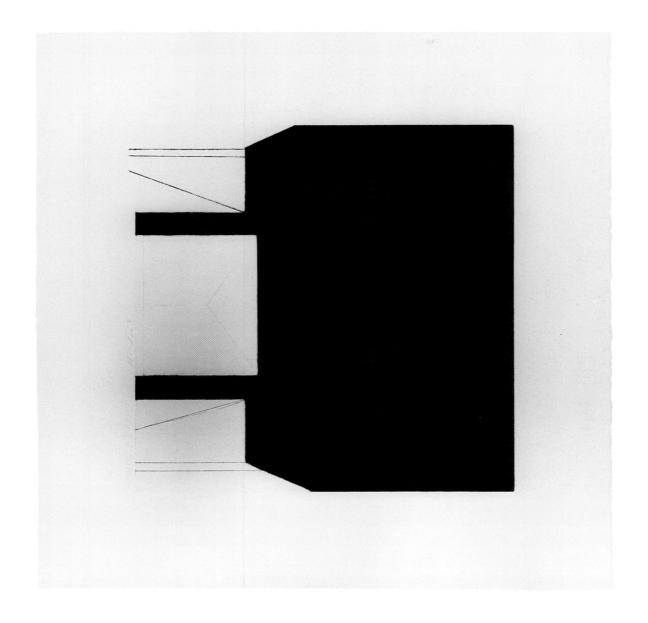

4. *Half Hats and Whole, March 24, 1979.* Aquatint with scraped and burnished areas, soft-ground, and
hard-ground. Printed in black from three plates. Note: one of the plates is 18¼ × 18¼ (46.4 × 46.4).

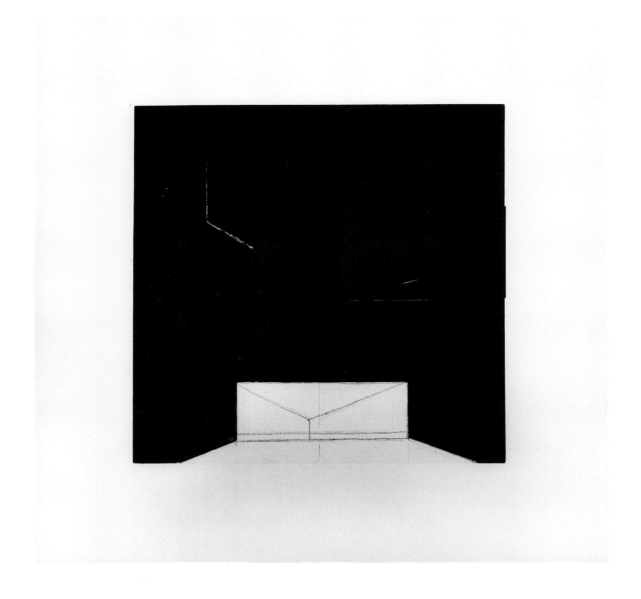

5. *Whole Hat and Halves, March 22, 1979.* Aquatint with scraped and burnished areas, soft-ground, and hard-ground. Printed in black from three plates.

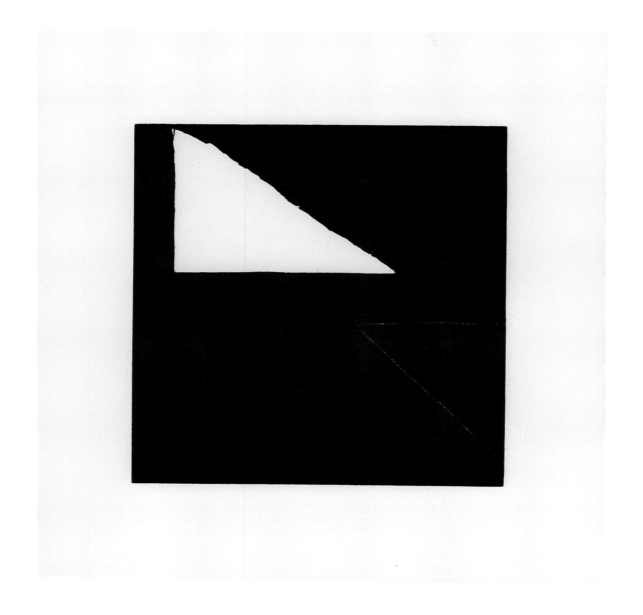

6. *Iceberg/Boat Prow, March 25, 1979*. Aquatint. Printed in black from two plates.

7. *Navel and Panties/Lake and Moon, March 26, 1979.* Aquatint with scraped and burnished areas and
hard-ground. Printed in black from one plate, on Don Farnsworth handmade paper with mohair.

8. *Cigarette/Stack, March 28, 1979.* Aquatint with scraped and burnished areas and hard-ground. Printed in black from one plate.

"Smokers," 1980.
Portfolio of three aquatints with scraped and burnished areas, drypoint, mezzotint, and hard-ground.
Each image printed in black from one 42 × 42 (106.7 × 106.7) copper plate on a sheet of 41½ × 41½ (105.4 × 105.4) Rolled Rives BFK paper.
Edition: Ten, plus ten artist's proofs, three trial proofs, and one right-to-print proof.
Printed by Hidekatsu Takada and Lilah Toland at Crown Point Press, Oakland, California.
Published by Parasol Press, New York.

9. Canyon/Pistol, Feb. 18, 1980.

10. *Cigarette/Stack, Feb. 20, 1980.*

11. *Cigarette, Feb. 26, 1980.*

12. *Canyon, Feb. 28, 1980.*
Aquatint with scraped and bur-
nished areas and hard-ground.
Printed in Thalo blue from one
42 × 42 (106.7 × 106.7) copper
plate on a sheet of 41½ × 41½
(105.4 × 105.4) Rolled Rives
BFK paper.
Edition: Ten, plus ten artist's
proofs, three trial proofs, and
one right-to-print proof.
Printed by Hidekatsu Takada
and Lilah Toland at Crown Point
Press, Oakland, California.
Published by Parasol Press,
New York.

"Tramp Pictures—Cypresses
and Stacks," 1982.
Portfolio of five linoleum cuts.
Edition: Fifteen, plus five artist's
proofs and two printer's proofs.
Printed by Claude Jinchat at
Imprimerie Arnéra, Vallauris,
France.
Published by Blum Helman
Gallery in collaboration with
Carmen Giménez, New York.

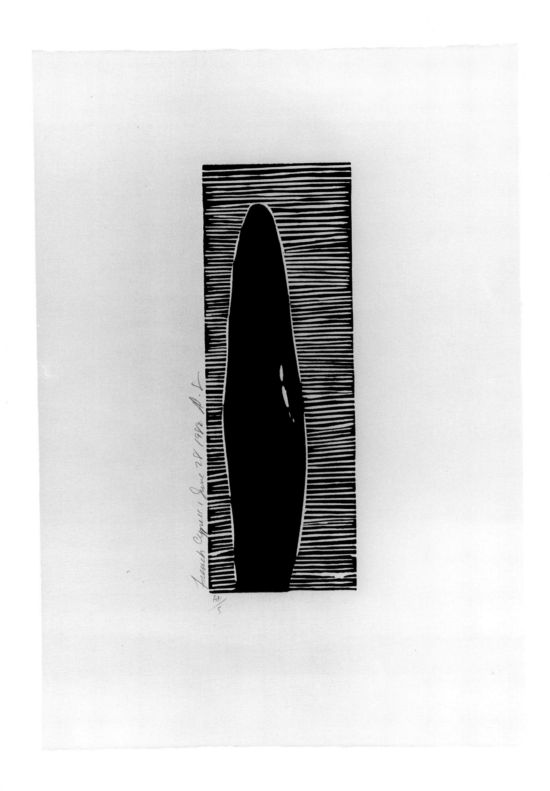

13. *French Cypress 1, June 28, 1982.* Printed in black from one 13⅞ × 4⅝ (35.3 × 11.8) linoleum block on a sheet of 22¼ × 15 (56.5 × 38.1) Arches Cover White paper.

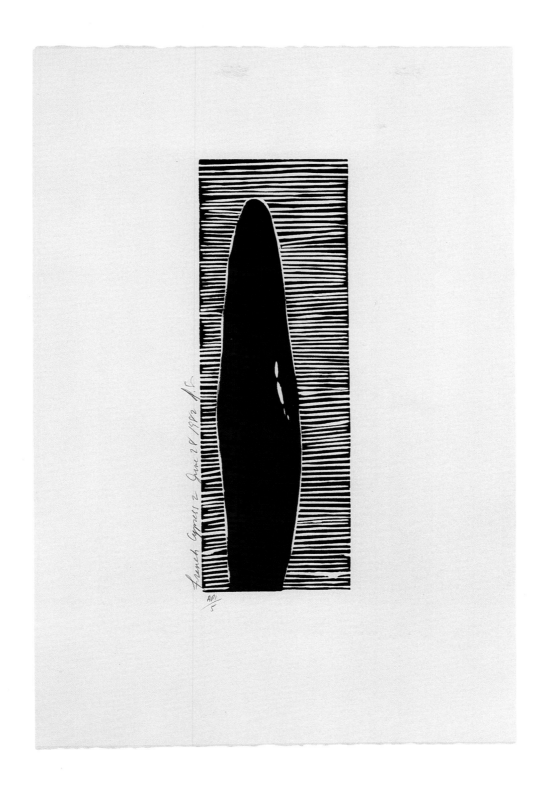

14. *French Cypress 2, June 28, 1982.* Printed in green from one 13⅞ × 4⅝ (35.3 × 11.8) linoleum block on a sheet of 22¼ × 15 (56.5 × 38.1) Arches Cover White paper.

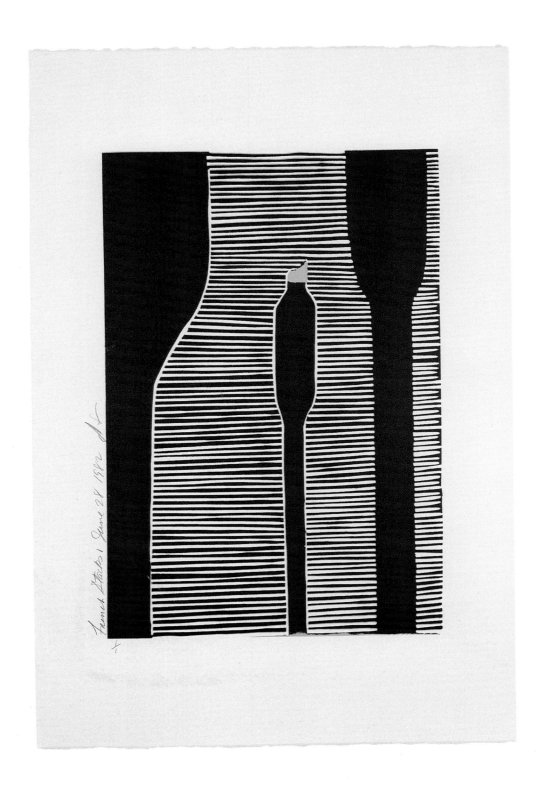

15. *French Stacks 1, June 28, 1982.* Printed in black and yellow from one 15½ × 10½ (39.4 × 26.7) linoleum block on a sheet of 22¼ × 15 (56.5 × 38.1) Arches Cover White paper.

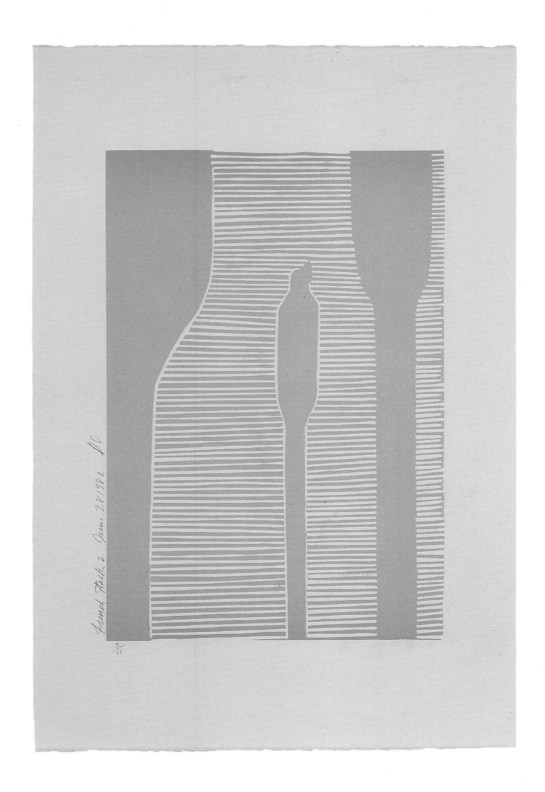

16. *French Stacks 2, June 28, 1982.* Printed in yellow from one 15½ × 10½ (39.4 × 26.7) linoleum block on a sheet of 22¼ × 15 (56.5 × 38.1) Arches Cover White paper.

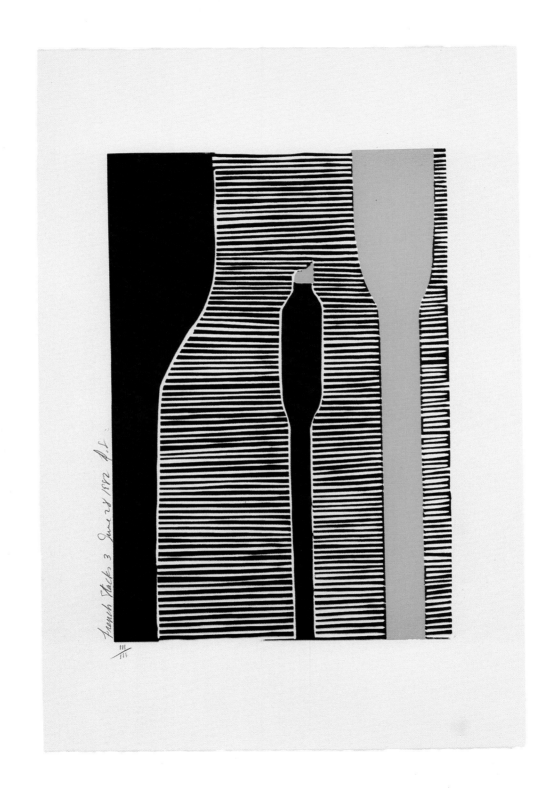

17. *French Stacks 3, June 28, 1982.* Printed in black and yellow from one 15½ × 10½ (39.4 × 26.7) linoleum block on a sheet of 22¼ × 15 (56.5 × 38.1) Arches Cover White paper.

"Tramp Pictures—Irises," 1982.
Portfolio of three linoleum cuts.
Each image printed from one
15½ × 10½ (39.4 × 26.7) linoleum
block on a sheet of 22¼ × 15
(56.5 × 38.1) Arches Cover White
paper.
Edition: Fifteen, plus five artist's
proofs and two printer's proofs.
Printed by Claude Jinchat at
Imprimerie Arnéra, Vallauris,
France.
Published by Blum Helman
Gallery in collaboration with
Carmen Giménez, New York.

18. *French Iris 1, June 28, 1982.* Printed in green.

19. *French Iris 2, June 28, 1982.* Printed in black and green.

20. *French Iris 3, June 28, 1982.* Printed in black and yellow.

"Black Tulips," 1983–84.
Portfolio of four aquatints.
Each image printed in black
from one 6 × 4 (15.2 × 10.2) steel-
faced copper plate on a sheet of
20¼ × 13¼ (51.4 × 33.7) Arches
555-pound paper.
Edition: Twenty, plus eight
artist's proofs, one printer's proof,
and one B.A.T.
Printed by Gregory Burnet and
Maurice Payne at I.M.E. Studios,
New York.
Published by Blum Helman
Gallery, New York.

21. *Black Tulip, Nov. 26, 1983.*

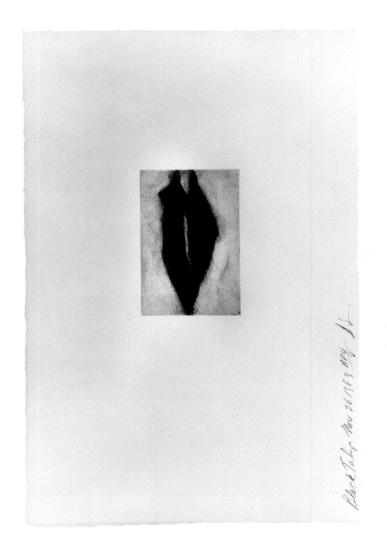

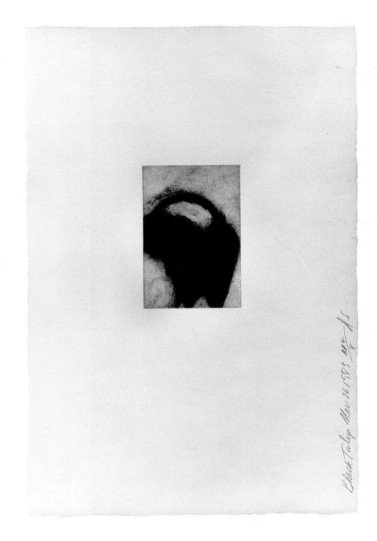

22. *Black Tulip, Nov. 26, 1983.*

23. *Black Tulip, Nov. 26, 1983.*

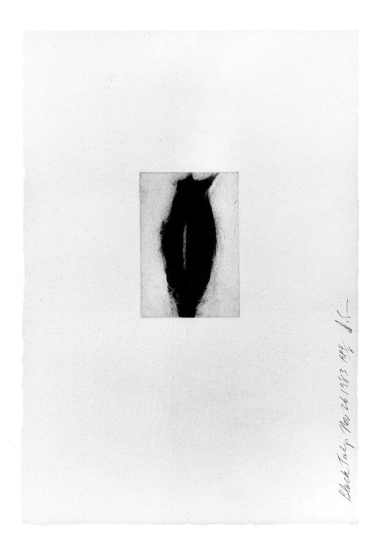

24. *Black Tulip, Nov. 26, 1983.*

"Black Lemons," 1984–85.
Portfolio of four aquatints
with open-bite.
Each image printed in black
from one 62 × 48 (157.5 × 121.9)
copper plate on a sheet of
62½ × 48½ (158.8 × 123.2)
Somerset Satin paper.
Edition: Ten, plus ten artist's
proofs and one right-to-print
proof.
Printed by Brenda Zlamany
and Joanne Howard at Jeryl
Parker Editions, New York.
Published by Parasol Press,
New York.

25. *Black Lemon, Nov. 28, 1984.*

"Still Life with Pears and Lemons," 1986.
Portfolio of one photolithograph in colors, one aquatint in black, and one overprinting of the aquatint plate with additional etching on the photolithograph. Aquatint printed from one 12 × 12 (30.5 × 30.5) copper plate. Photolithograph, aquatint, and composite are each printed on a 24½ × 21 (62.2 × 53.3) sheet of Somerset Satin paper.
Edition: Forty-five, plus ten artist's proofs.
Aquatint printed by Jeryl Parker Editions, New York; photolithograph printed by Maurice Sanchez at Derriere L'Etoile Studio, New York.
Published by Parasol Press, New York.

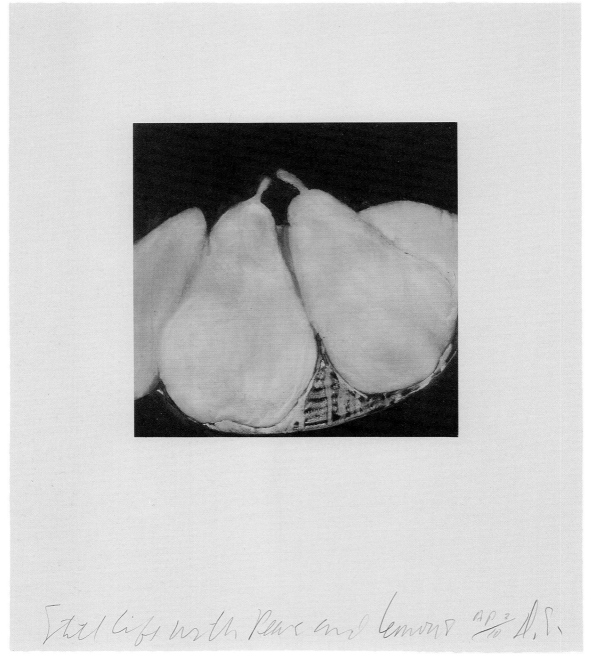

26. *Still Life with Pears and Lemons.*

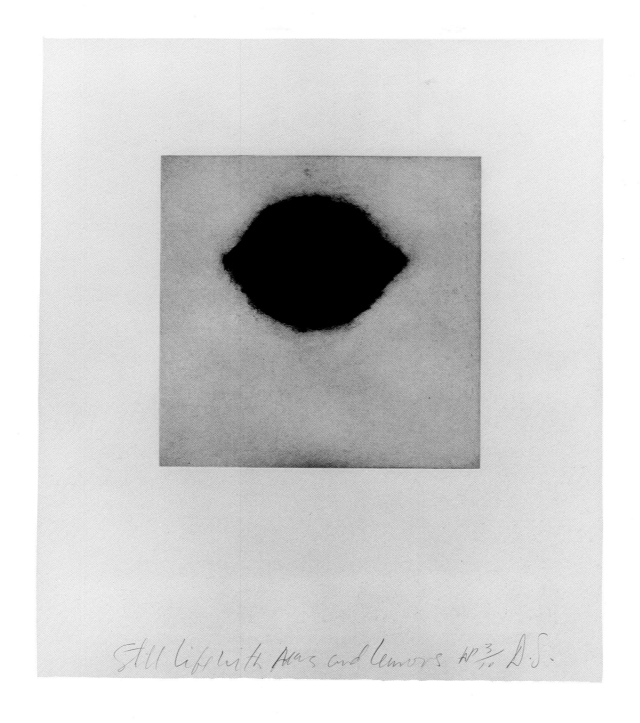

27. *Still Life with Pears and Lemons.*

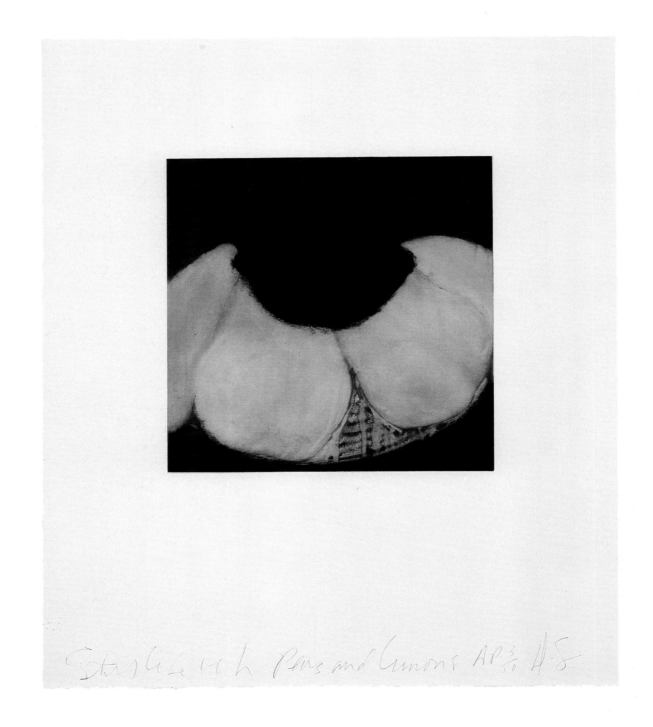

28. *Still Life with Pears and Lemons.*

29. *Black Tulips and Lemons, Nov. 28, 1986,* 1986–87.
Aquatint.
Printed in black from one 15 × 21 (38.1 × 53.3) copper plate on a 22 × 30 (55.9 × 76.2) sheet of Arches Watercolor paper.
Edition: Fifty-four, plus nine artist's proofs, one printer's proof, and one B.A.T.
Printed by Gregory Burnet and Maurice Payne at I.M.E. Studios, New York.
Published by the Jewish Museum, New York.

"Freesias," 1987.
Portfolio of six aquatints.
Each image printed in black
from one 14½ × 15½ (36.8 × 39.4)
copper plate on a sheet of
19½ × 20 (49.5 × 50.8) Arches
Cover White paper.
Edition: Forty, plus eleven artist's
proofs and six printer's proofs.
Printed by Aldo Crommelynck at
Aldo Crommelynck Studio, Paris.
Published by Pace Editions,
Inc., New York.

30. *Freesia, April 7, 1987.*

31. *Freesia, April 10, 1987.*

32. *Freesia, April 15, 1987.*

33. Freesia, April 16, 1987.

"Lemons," 1987.
Portfolio of four aquatints.
Each image printed in black
from one 62 × 48 (157.5 × 121.9)
copper plate on a sheet of
62¾ × 49¼ (159.4 × 125.1)
Somerset Satin paper.
Edition: Fourteen, plus
ten artist's proofs and six
printer's proofs.
Printed by Carol Weaver, Felix
Harlan, and Jeryl Parker at Jeryl
Parker Editions, New York.
Published by Parasol Press,
New York.

34. *Black Lemons and Egg, April 14, 1987.*

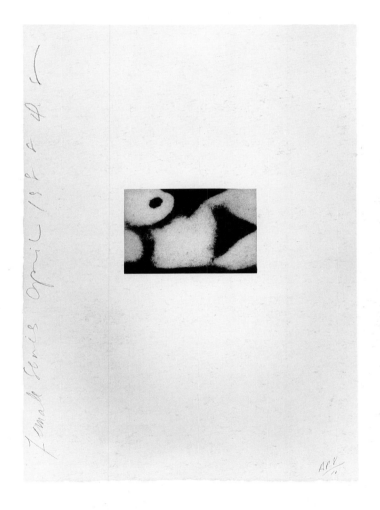

"Female Series, April 1988," 1988.
Portfolio of eleven aquatints.
Each image printed in black
from one 6 × 4 (15.2 × 10.2)
copper plate on a sheet of
21¼ × 15 (54 × 38.1) Arches
Watercolor paper.
Edition: Fifteen, plus ten artist's
proofs, two trial proofs, and one
right-to-print proof.
Printed by Felix Harlan and
Carol Weaver at Harlan-Weaver
Intaglio, New York.
Published by Parasol Press,
New York.

35. *Female Series, April 1988.*

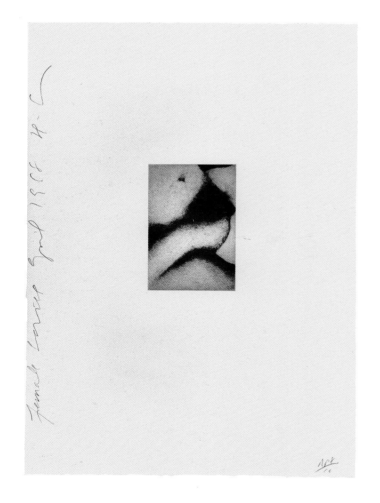

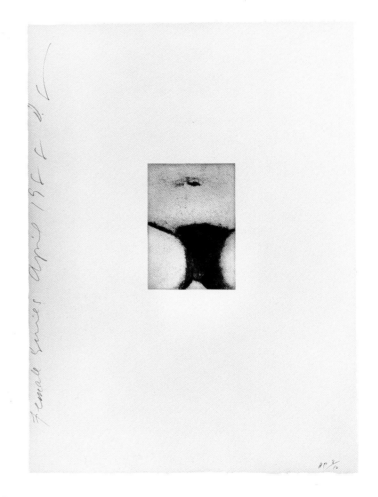

36. *Female Series, April 1988.*

37. *Female Series, April 1988.*

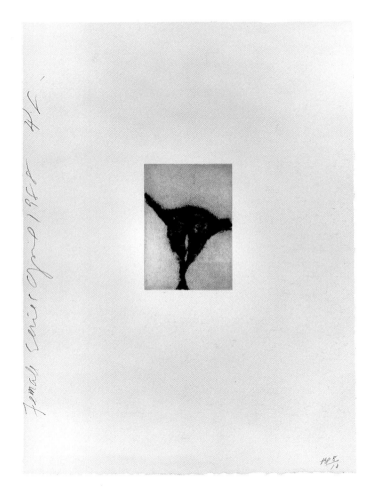

38. *Female Series, April 1988.*

39. *Female Series, April 1988.*

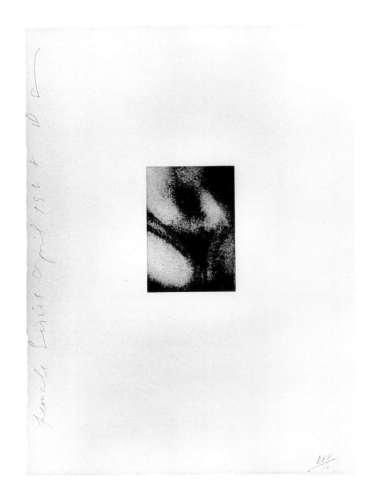

40. *Female Series, April 1988.*   41. *Female Series, April 1988.*

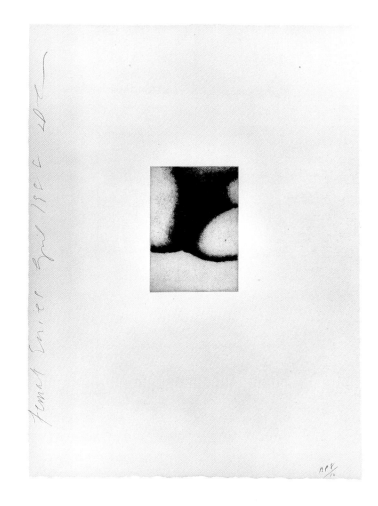

42. *Female Series, April 1988.*

43. *Female Series, April 1988.*

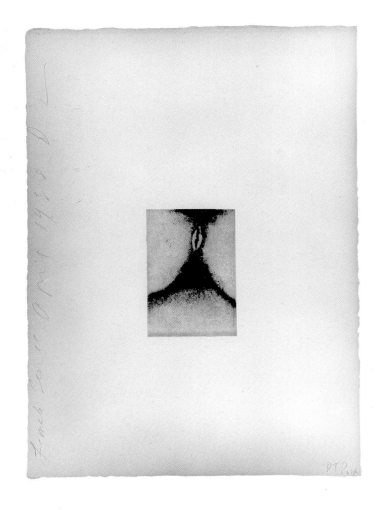

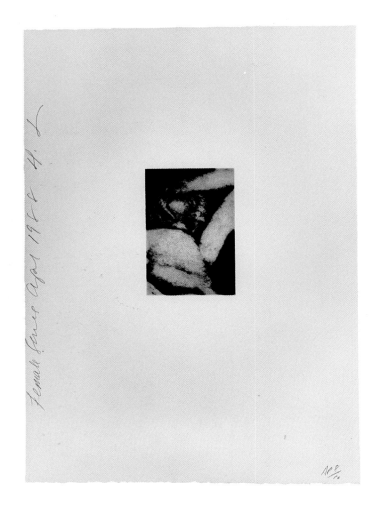

44. *Female Series, April 1988.*

45. *Female Series, April 1988.*

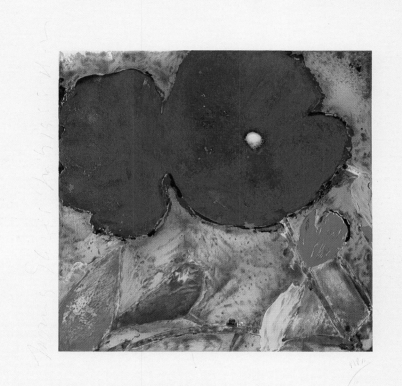

46. *Morning Glories, July 1988,* 1988.
Screenprint.
Image printed in forty-five
colors from forty-five 12 × 12
(30.5 × 30.5) screens on a sheet
of 23 × 22 (58.4 × 55.9) Arches
88 paper.
Edition: One hundred, plus ten
artist's proofs, four printer's
proofs, three trial proofs, and
one right-to-print proof.
Printed by Katsumi Suzuki and
Takeshi Arita at Watanabe
Studio, New York.
Published by Parasol Press,
New York.

47. *Quince, Sept. 7, 1988,* 1988.
Screenprint.
Image printed in fifty-six colors
from fifty-six 12½ × 12¼
(31.8 × 31.1) screens on a sheet
of 23 × 22 (58.4 × 55.9) Arches
88 paper.
Edition: One hundred, plus
fifteen artist's proofs and four
printer's proofs.
Printed by Jo Watanabe at
Watanabe Studio, New York.
Published by the Metropolitan
Museum of Art, New York.

48. *Four Pears, Feb. 1989*, 1989.
Screenprint.
Image printed in forty-eight
colors from forty-eight 12 × 12
(30.5 × 30.5) screens on a sheet
of 23 × 22 (58.4 × 55.9) Arches
88 paper.
Edition: One hundred, plus
fifteen artist's proofs, four print-
er's proofs, and three trial proofs.
Printed by Katsumi Suzuki and
Takeshi Arita at Watanabe
Studio, New York.
Published by the Metropolitan
Museum of Art, New York.

49. *Peppers, May 30, 1989*, 1989.
Screenprint.
Image printed in fifty colors
from fifty 12 × 12 (30.5 × 30.5)
screens on a sheet of 23 × 22
(58.4 × 55.9) Arches 88 paper.
Edition: One hundred, plus ten
artist's proofs, six printer's
proofs, and four trial proofs.
Printed by Katsumi Suzuki at
Watanabe Studio, New York.
Published by Parasol Press,
New York.

"Fruits and Flowers," 1991.
Portfolio of eight screenprints.
Each image printed from 12 × 12
(30.5 × 30.5) screens on a sheet
of 23 × 22 (58.4 × 55.9) Arches
88 paper.
Edition: One hundred twenty-
five, plus twenty artist's proofs.
Printed by Katsumi Suzuki and
Robert Meyer at Watanabe
Studio, New York.
Published by Parasol Press,
New York.

50. *Flowers, Aug. 1989.* Printed in forty-two colors from forty-two screens.

51. *Fish, Aug. 1990.* Printed in eleven colors from eleven screens.

"Lip Prints, Oct. 1989," 1989.
Portfolio of four aquatints.
Each image printed in black
from one 3 × 4¼ (7.6 × 10.8)
copper plate on a sheet of
13 × 10 (33 × 25.4) Rives BFK
paper.
Edition: One hundred, plus
twenty-five artist's proofs and
four *hors commerce*.
Printed by Aldo Crommelynck
at Aldo Crommelynck Studio,
Paris.
Published by Editions de la
Difference, Paris.

52. *Lip Prints, Oct. 1989.*

53. *Lip Prints, Oct. 1989.*

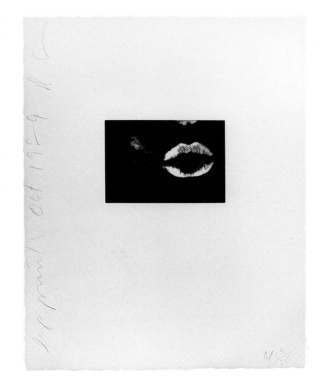

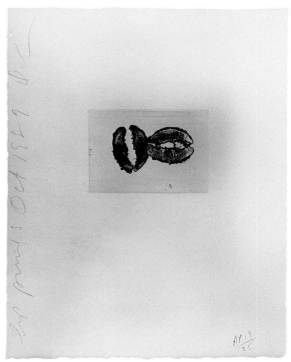

54. *Lip Prints, Oct. 1989.* 55. *Lip Prints, Oct. 1989.*

"Black Roses, Dec. 1989,"
1989–90.
Portfolio of three aquatints.
Each image printed in black
from one 22 × 30 (55.9 × 76.2)
copper plate on a sheet of
32 × 39½ (81.3 × 100.3) Twin-
rocker handmade paper with DS
watermark.
Edition: Fifty-three, plus ten
artist's proofs and one B.A.T.
Printed by Gregory Burnet and
Maurice Payne at I.M.E. Studios,
New York.
Published by Parasol Press,
New York.

56. *Black Roses, Oct. 1989.*

57. *Black Roses, Nov. 1989.*

58. Black Roses, Dec. 1989.

59. *Black Roses, May 1990*, 1990.
Screenprint.
Image printed in seven colors
from seven 34 × 55½ (86.4 × 141)
screens on a sheet of 34 × 55½
(86.4 × 141) Somerset Satin
White paper.
Edition: One hundred, plus
fifteen artist's proofs and five
printer's proofs.
Printed by Jo Watanabe, Goro
Fujit, and Robert Meyer at
Watanabe Studio, New York.
Published by Parasol Press,
New York.

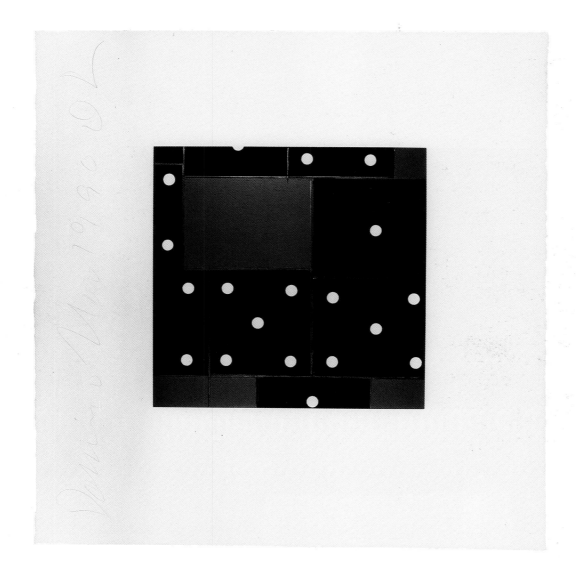

"Dominoes," 1990–91.
Portfolio of three screenprints.
Each image printed in four colors from four 12 × 12 (30.5 × 30.5) screens on a sheet of 23½ × 22½ (59.7 × 57.2) Arches 88 paper.
Edition: One hundred, plus twenty-five artist's proofs, four printer's proofs, and one right-to-print proof.
Printed by Hidemi Nomura at Watanabe Studio, New York.
Published by Editions Portmanteau Press, New York, and Diffusion Art Multi, Paris.

60. *Dominoes, Nov. 1990.*

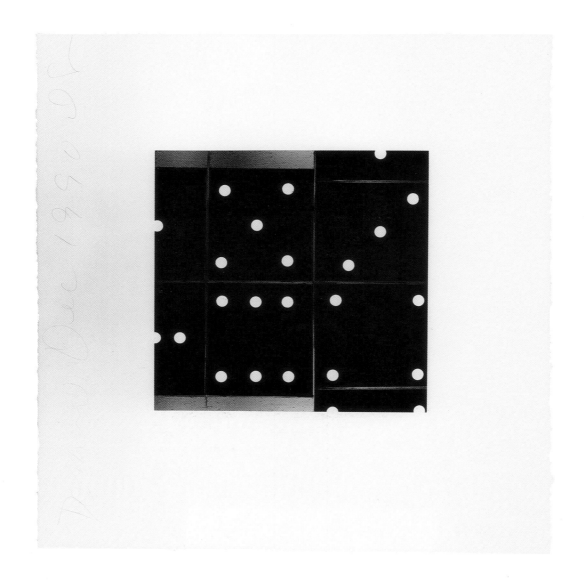

61. *Dominoes, Dec. 1990.*

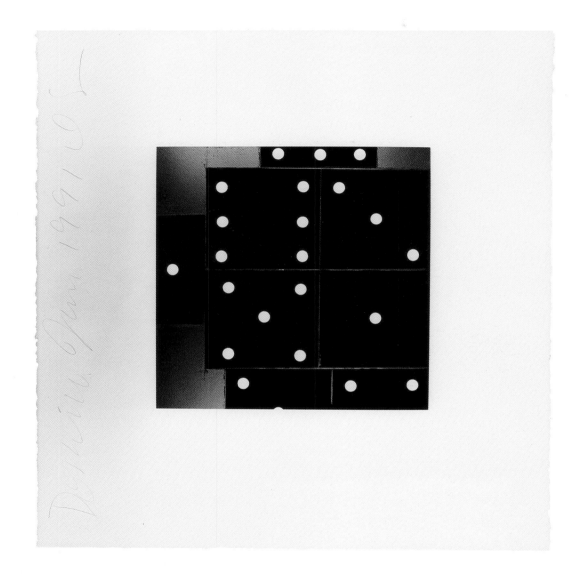

62. *Dominoes, Jan. 1991.*

"Pomegranates," 1990.
Portfolio of three aquatints.
Each image printed in black
from one 40 × 30 (101.6 × 76.2)
copper plate on a sheet of
48 × 36 (121.9 × 91.4) Somerset
White paper.
Edition: Sixty, plus thirteen
artist's proofs and one B.A.T.
Printed by Gregory Burnet and
Maurice Payne at I.M.E. Studios,
New York.
Published by Waddington
Graphics, London.

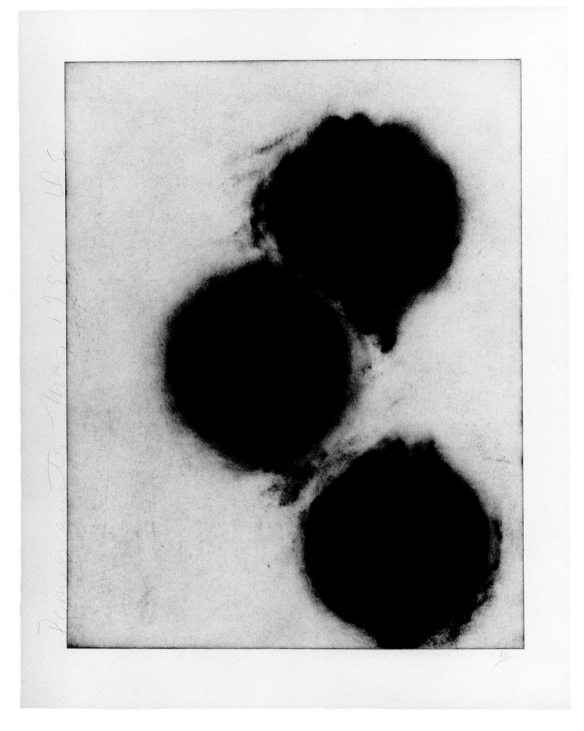

63. *Pomegranates, May 1990.*

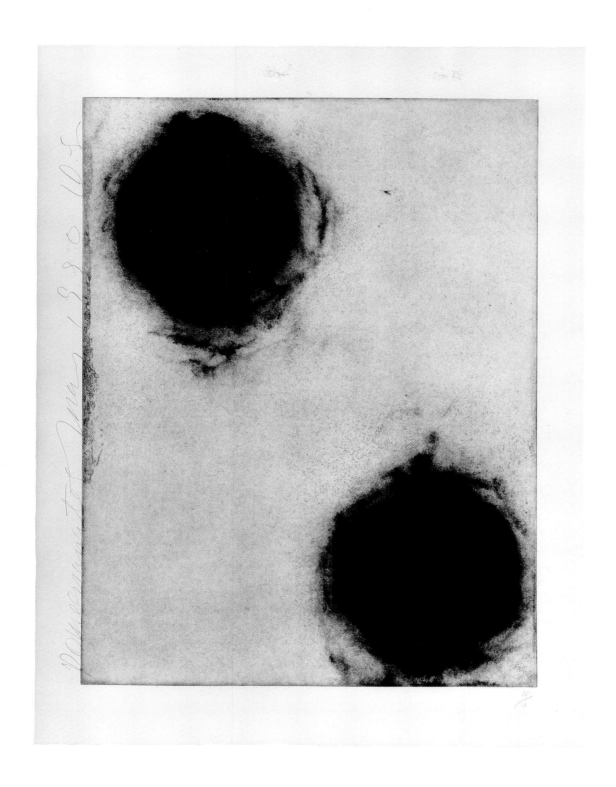

64. *Pomegranates, May 1990.*

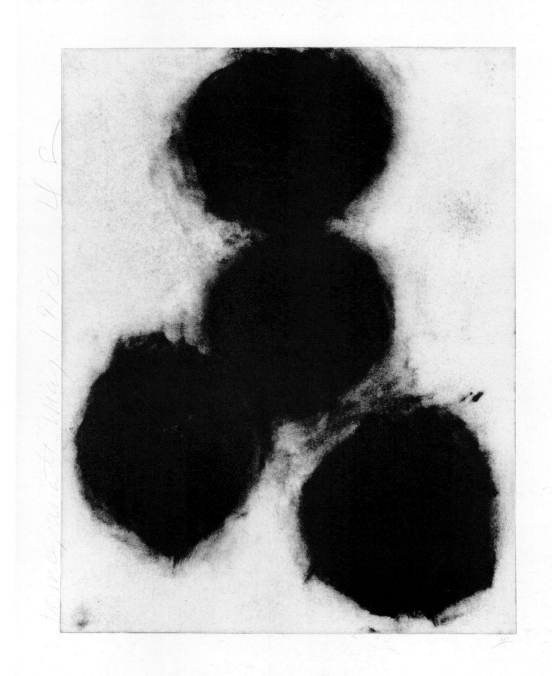

65. *Pomegranates, May 1990.*

"Morning Glories," 1991.
Portfolio of three aquatints.
Each image printed in black
from one 60 × 48 (152.4 × 121.9)
copper plate on a sheet of
62 × 50 (157.5 × 127) Somerset
English 100 rag white paper.
Edition: Sixty, plus thirteen
artist's proofs and one B.A.T.
Printed by Gregory Burnet and
Maurice Payne at I.M.E. Studios,
New York.
Published by Waddington
Graphics, London.

66. *Morning Glories, Jan. 31, 1990.*

67. Morning Glories, Feb. 3, 1991.

68. *Morning Glories, Feb. 5, 1991.*

"Dominoes, Aug. 1990," 1990.
Portfolio of twenty-eight
aquatints with etching.
Each image printed in black
from one 11½ × 8 (29.2 × 20.3)
copper plate on a sheet of
21¼ × 15 (54 × 38.1) Twinrocker
handmade paper.
Edition: Fifty-three, plus ten
artist's proofs and one B.A.T.
Printed by Gregory Burnet and
Michael Payne at I.M.E. Studios,
New York, and editioned by
Richard Spare at Wellington
Studios, London.
Published by Parasol Press,
New York.

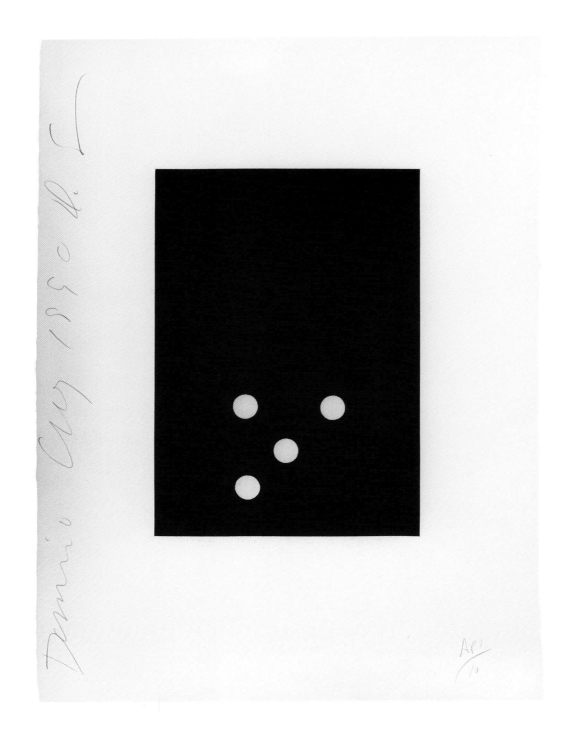

69. Domino, Aug. 1990.

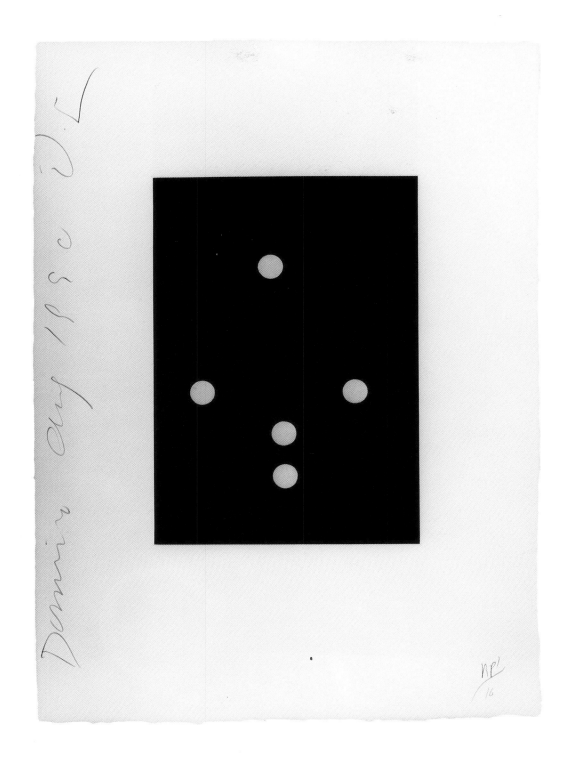

70. *Domino, Aug. 1990.*

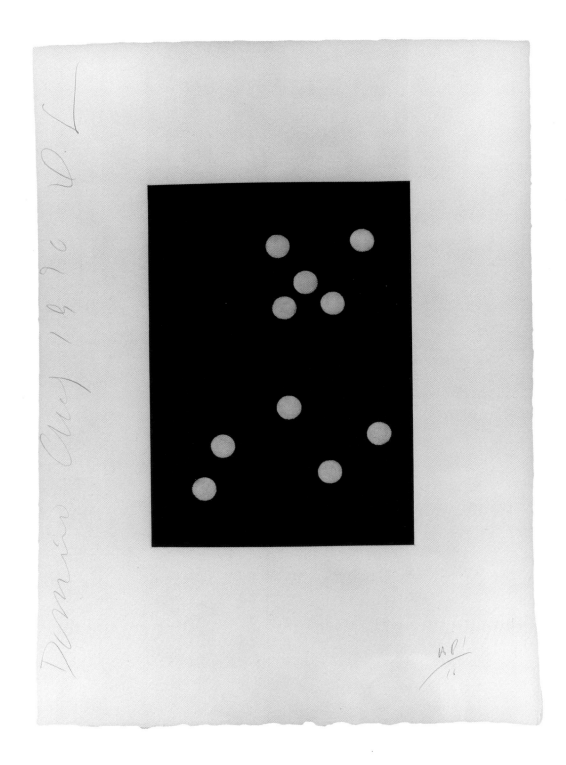

71. *Domino, Aug. 1990.*

72. *Domino, Aug. 1990.*

"Playing Cards," 1990.
Portfolio of fifty-four aquatints with etching.
Each image printed in black or red, corresponding to the suits, from one 11½ × 8 (29.2 × 20.3) copper plate on a sheet of 20⅞ × 15 (53 × 38.1) Twinrocker handmade paper.
Edition: Forty-four, plus ten artist's proofs and one B.A.T.
Printed by Gregory Burnet and Maurice Payne at I.M.E. Studios, New York, and editioned by Richard Spare at Wellington Studios, London.
Published by Parasol Press, New York.

73. *Red Joker, Sept. 10, 1990.*

74. *Ten of Spades, Aug. 2, 1990.*

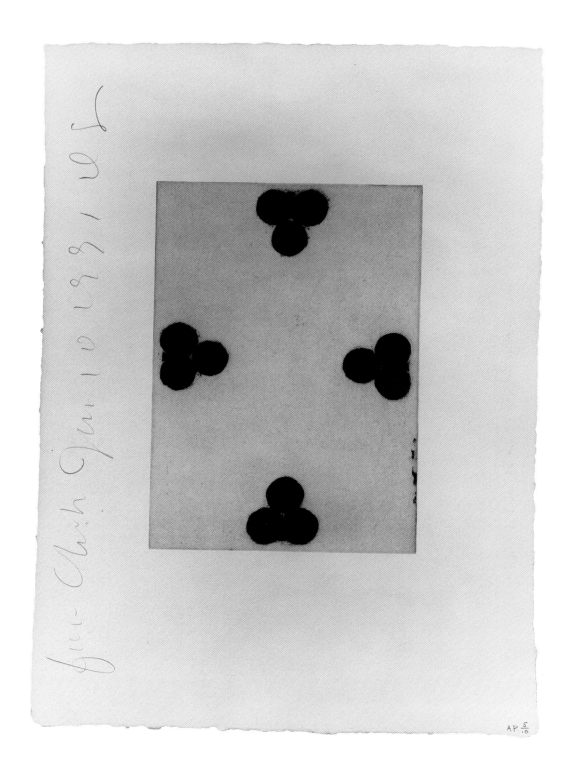

75. Four of Clubs, Jan. 10, 1991.

76. *Ten of Diamonds, April 3, 1991.*

77. Eight of Clubs, Dec. 22, 1990.

78. Seven of Spades, Aug. 7, 1990.

79. *Seven of Diamonds, May 6, 1990.*

80. *King of Hearts, Mar. 5, 1990.*

"Warm and Cold," 1985.
Book in portfolio format with
nine lithographs (eight of which
are handcolored with watercolor) and two photographs.
Text by David Mamet.
Image sizes vary.
Each spread (two images)
printed on a sheet of 21 × 34
(53.3 × 86.4) Arches 300-gram
paper.
Edition: One hundred, plus
twenty artist's proofs, two
printer's proofs, two publisher's
proofs, and one right-to-print
proof.
Printed by Arnold Samet,
Tracey Regester, and Judith
Solodkin; handcolored by
Cinda Sparling at Solo Press,
New York.
Published by Fawbush Editions
and Solo Press, New York.

If you are far away from home

81. "If you are far away from home"

A keepsake will remind you of those who love you

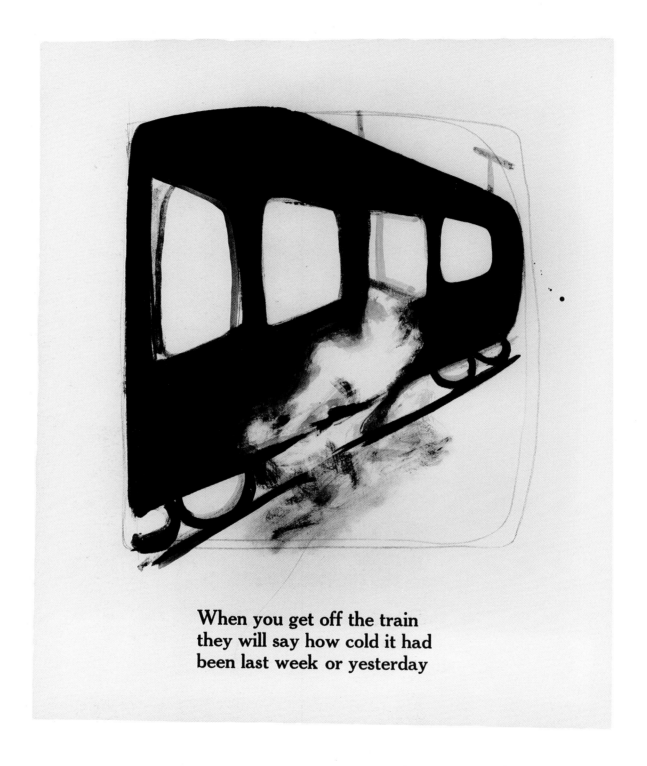

**When you get off the train
they will say how cold it had
been last week or yesterday**

83. "When you get off the train
they will say how cold it had
been last week or yesterday"

**And I want to sit in the cafe
It's warm there and the people
speak to one another earnestly**

84. "And I want to sit in the cafe
It's warm there and the people
speak to one another earnestly"

CHRONOLOGY

This chronology lists Sultan's one-person exhibitions, as well as other major facts of his life.

1951   Born in Asheville, North Carolina.

1973   Receives B.F.A., University of North Carolina.

1975   Receives M.F.A., School of Art Institute, Chicago.

1976   Chicago, N.A.M.E. Gallery.

1977   *February 2–26*. New York, Artists Space.

October 20–November 27. Long Island City, New York, P.S. 1 and the Clocktower Gallery, The Institute for Contemporary Art, Special Projects Room, *Turning the Room Sideways*.

1978-79   Receives Creative Artists Public Service Grant, New York.

1979   *February 24–March 2*. New York, Willard Gallery, *Donald Sultan*.

November 9–December 12. Chicago, Young Hoffman Gallery, *Donald Sultan*.

1980   *October 4–30*. New York, Willard Gallery. *Donald Sultan*.

1980-81   Receives grant from National Endowment for the Arts.

1981   *February 4–28*. San Francisco, Dan Weinberg Gallery, *Donald Sultan: Recent Paintings*.

1982   *April 14–May 8*. New York, Blum Helman Gallery, *Donald Sultan*.

October 14–November 13. Düsseldorf, Hans Strelow Gallery, *Donald Sultan: Bilder und Zeichnungen*.

1983   *May 12–May 31*. Tokyo, Akira Ikeda Gallery, *Donald Sultan*.

1984   *February 8–March 3*. New York, Blum Helman Gallery, *Donald Sultan: New Paintings*.

1985   *April 3–27*. New York, Blum Helman Gallery, *Donald Sultan: New Paintings*.

October 5–30. Boston, Barbara Krakow Gallery, *Donald Sultan: Prints 1979–1985*. Travels to: Georgia State University, Atlanta; Baxter Gallery, Portland School of Art, Maine; Wesleyan University, Middletown, Connecticut; Asheville Art Museum, North Carolina; and California State University, Long Beach.

1985-86   *November 29, 1985–January 4, 1986*. New York, Blum Helman Gallery, *Donald Sultan: Small Paintings*.

December 20, 1985–January 17, 1986. Rome, Gian Enzo Sperone Gallery, *Donald Sultan*.

1986   *April 2–26*. New York, Blum Helman Gallery, *Donald Sultan*.

April 5–26. New York, Blum Helman Gallery, *Donald Sultan: Drawings*.

May 1–June 24. San Francisco, A.P. Gianni Gallery, Bank of America, World Headquarters, *Donald Sultan: A Survey*.

October 16–November 8. Paris, Galerie Montenay-Desol, *Donald Sultan*.

October 21–November 22. Paris, Galerie de L'estampe Contemporaine Bibliothèque Nationale, Rostonde Colbert, *Donald Sultan: gravures monumentales*.

1986-87   *November 8, 1986–January 3, 1987*. St. Louis, The Greenberg Gallery, *Donald Sultan: Drawings and Paintings*.

1987   *February 7–28*. Nagoya, Japan, Akira Ikeda Gallery, *Donald Sultan Paintings*.

New York, Blum Helman Gallery, *Donald Sultan Cigarette Paintings 1980–81 and Photographs 1985–86*.

March 11–April 11. Santa Monica, Blum Helman Gallery, *Donald Sultan: Recent Paintings*.

November 4–28. New York, Blum Helman Gallery, *Donald Sultan: Recent Painting*.

November 7–December 2. Boston, Barbara Krakow Gallery, *Small Paintings: Small Drawings*

November 11–December 9. Rome, Gian Enzo Sperone Gallery, *Donald Sultan*.

1987-88   *November 24, 1987–January 10, 1988*. Chicago, Museum of Contemporary Art, *Donald Sultan*. Catalogue. Travels to: Los Angeles Museum of Contemporary Art; Fort Worth Art Museum, Texas; and the Brooklyn Museum, New York.

December 3, 1987–January 3, 1988. Seattle, Greg Kucera Gallery, *Black Lemons-Recent Prints*.

1988   *January 22–February 27*. New York, Martina Hamilton and Associates, *Donald Sultan Prints and Drawings*.

February 4–May 3. New York, Museum of Modern Art, *Donald Sultan: Black Lemons*.

October 6–29. Paris, Galerie Montenay, *Donald Sultan*.

October 7–November 5. Lausanne, Switzerland, La Galerie Alice Pauli, *Donald Sultan*.

1989   *March 20–April 29*. Santa Monica, Blum Helman Gallery, *Donald Sultan Sculpture*.

April 27–June 4. New York, Paul Kasmin Gallery, *Donald Sultan Playing Cards Drawings*.

May 4–June 16. London, Runkle-Hue-Williams Ltd., *Donald Sultan Works on Paper.* Catalogue.

September 8–November 4. St. Louis, The Greenberg Gallery, *Donald Sultan: New Sculpture.*

September 12–October 5. New York, M. Knoedler & Company, *Donald Sultan: Drawings.*

November 18–December 23. New York, Richard Green Gallery, *Donald Sultan: A Selection of Prints.*

1990   *April 28–May 4.* New York, M. Knoedler & Company, *Donald Sultan: Paintings.* Catalogue.

June 7–July 1. Seattle, Greg Kucera Gallery, *Donald Sultan Screen Prints and Etchings.*

October 11–November 3. Vancouver, Canada, Equinox Gallery, *Donald Sultan.*

November 28–December 21. London, Waddington Galleries, *Donald Sultan.*

1991   *January 8–February 9.* San Francisco, John Berggruen Gallery, *Donald Sultan—Paintings, Drawings, and Prints.*

January 10–February 13. New York, Mary Ryan Gallery, *Donald Sultan, Recent Print Projects: Dominoes, Fruits and Flowers, Playing Cards.*

January 12–February 9. New York, M. Knoedler & Company, *Donald Sultan: Sculpture.*

March 14–April 6. Houston, Meredith Long and Co., *Donald Sultan: Drawings—Paintings.*

April 4–28. Seattle, Greg Kucera Gallery, *Donald Sultan: Dominoes, Playing Cards, Fruit and Flowers.*

September 13–October 12. Santa Monica, Richard Green Gallery, *Donald Sultan.*

1992   *January 25–February 25.* Birmingham, Michigan, Hill Gallery, *Donald Sultan: Drawings.*

March 21–April 25. New York, M. Knoedler & Company, *Donald Sultan: Paintings.*

Baer, Brigitte. *Donald Sultan's Black Lemons.* Exhibition brochure. New York: The Museum of Modern Art, 1988.

Cathcart, Linda. *The Americans: The Landscape.* Exhibition catalogue. Houston: Contemporary Arts Museum, 1981.

Christov-Barkargiev, Carolyn. "Donald Sultan." Interview. *Flash Art.* June 1986; pp. 48–50.

Combes, Chantal. *The New Romantic Landscape.* Exhibition catalogue. Stamford, Connecticut: The Whitney Museum of American Art, 1987.

Dunlop, Ian, and Lynne Warren. *Donald Sultan.* Exhibition catalogue. Chicago: Museum of Contemporary Art, 1987.

Friedman, Ceil. *Donald Sultan: Prints 1979–1985.* Exhibition catalogue. Boston: Barbara Krakow Gallery, 1985.

Goldwater, Marge, et al. *Images and Impressions: Painters Who Print.* Exhibition catalogue. Minneapolis: Walker Art Center, 1984.

Henry, Gerrit. "Donald Sultan: His Prints." *The Print Collector's Newsletter.* January-February 1986, pp. 193–196.

Henry, Gerrit. "Dark Poetry," *ARTnews,* April 1987, pp. 104–111.

Linker, Kate, et al. *Individuals: A Selected History of Contemporary Art, 1945–1986.* New York: Abbeville Press; Los Angeles: The Museum of Contemporary Art, 1986.

Rapko, J., and C. N. McCann. "At the Point of Paradox." Interview. *Artweek.* February 7, 1991, pp. 14–15.

Rose, Barbara. *Sultan: An Interview with Donald Sultan by Barbara Rose.* New York: Vintage Books, 1988.

Walker, Barry. *Public and Private: American Prints Today—The 24th National Print Exhibition.* Brooklyn, New York: The Brooklyn Museum, 1986, p. 122.